Awakening
to
Self-Love

A Collection of Poems on Overcoming Limiting Beliefs, Embracing Authenticity, Finding Freedom and Inner Joy

Velory Irungbam

Dedication

*I would like to dedicate this book to all the individuals who are actively en-gaged in **self-healing** and **self-improvement**, who may be experiencing stagnation in one or more areas of their lives, and who are seeking guidance on how to achieve personal growth. I also extend this dedication to those who embody the principles of self-love and serve as beacons of light, elevating the collective consciousness.*

Contents

Introduction

*"Your task is not to seek for love, but merely to seek
and find all the barriers within yourself that you
have built against it." – Rumi*

"Awakening to Self-Love" is a captivating collection of poems that chronicles my personal journey toward self-love, a journey that I hope will inspire and empower readers to embark on their own. For years, I searched for love outside of myself, not realizing that the true source of love lies within.

*"I have lived on the lip of insanity, wanting to know
the reasons, knocking on a door. It opens. I've been
knocking from the inside!" -Rumi*

In a world where the pressure to be perfect is constantly present, it can be difficult to remember that we are all imperfect and that is okay. We often hold ourselves to unrealistic standards, leading to a negative self-image and a sense of inadequacy. This can have a detrimental effect on our mental and emotional well-being, making it hard for us to enjoy our lives and love ourselves.

Marissa Peer, in one of her Mindvalley Quests, "Uncompromised Life," mentions that "the feeling of not enough" is the common denominator of all human suffering and difficulties. And these limiting beliefs are the very reason why people strive to find their fulfillment through over-shopping, over-drinking, over-working, chasing love, fame, money, material success, food, etc.

Limiting beliefs, such as feeling not good enough, not beautiful enough, not lovable enough, not smart enough, not intelligent enough, not deserving enough, not talented enough, etc. which plagued me for much of my life, preventing me from fully showing up and embracing my authentic self. I struggled with perfectionism, fear of rejection, and abandonment, never realizing that my childhood experiences had shaped these beliefs. As a child, we have no control over how we picked up the limiting beliefs nor our caregivers were aware of the value of creating a safe environment especially emotionally, but as an adult, we have the responsibility to change these limiting beliefs.

To break the barrier of these limiting beliefs and cultivate self-love, it's important to identify and challenge these beliefs in order to overcome them. We need to heal our inner child wounds. We need to acknowledge our imperfections and embrace them as a part of our unique identity.

Though it is easy to lose sight of our own needs and priorities in today's fast-paced and changing world, we need to learn to be kinder and more compassionate towards ourselves, treating ourselves with the same care and understanding that we would offer to a dear friend. We must learn to treat ourselves with empathy and gentleness, especially during difficult times when we feel flawed and imperfect. Surrounding ourselves with affirmative individuals, like supportive friends and family, while minimizing exposure to toxic relationships and negative influences can help us in our self-love journey.

The journey to self-love is not an easy one, but the essential path toward our personal growth and overall wellness. It is an ongoing journey that demands consistent effort and practice. It requires us to confront our fears, doubts, and insecurities and to embrace our unique qualities, flaws, and imperfections. It takes courage, vulnerability, and a deep sense of self-awareness.

Self-love is not selfish and it's just not about accepting ourselves as we are, but also; about striving for growth and personal development. It's about setting healthy boundaries by saying no to things that don't serve us and saying yes to experiences and opportunities that bring us joy and fulfillment.

It's also important to remember that self-love is not just an individual pursuit, but a collective one. By cultivating self-love, we become better equipped to show compassion and kindness to others and to contribute positively to our communities and society as a whole.

> *Jay Shetty, in "8 Rules of Love" says "Self-Love is the foundation for all other love, and it starts with acknowledging and embracing your own worthiness. When you love and accept yourself, you open up the possibility for deeper connections and more meaningful relationships with others."*

Each poem within these pages is a reflection of my journey toward self-love and acceptance. Through the exploration of inner dialogue, relationships, self-worth, and self-acceptance, these poems offer a refreshing perspective on the transformative power of self-love. They also offer insights gained from my personal journey towards daily self-love practices, which have improved my self-esteem, self-confidence, and self-reliance, ultimately leading to more fulfilling relationships and a more satisfying life.

Through the art of poetry, I have found a powerful tool for processing complex emotions, practicing introspection, and gaining heightened self-awareness. I have come to recognize that societal conditioning and upbringing often lead us to reject aspects of ourselves and project insecurities onto others, which ultimately; undermines our well-being. My work also delves into the persistence of early childhood narratives into adulthood and intimate relationships, where we may blame others for our unfulfilled needs and desires. I hope to inspire readers to explore their inner selves through creative writing, journaling, or other forms of artistic expression that work for them.

Whether you are just beginning your journey to self-love or have been on this path for some time, "Awakening to Self-Love" offers a space for reflection, inspiration, and guidance. This book encourages readers to let go of self-doubt, fear, and insecurity, and to embrace self-love, confidence, and self-acceptance. It is a powerful reminder that we all deserve to give ourselves the love we need to grow and to allow others to show up fully in our lives.

Also, I invite readers who are seeking a fulfilling life, personal growth, and self-discovery to explore the transformative power of self-love in this book. By embracing self-love as a vital component of spiritual evolution and personal development, we can overcome the pervasive sense of not being good enough and bring peace and unity to the world. Through daily practice, we can raise our individual and collective consciousness, and create a more harmonious and loving world. May this book inspire and bless you on your journey toward greater self-love and fulfillment.

Let this book be your friend that walks beside you, saying *"You are not alone in this journey"* as you embark on your journey of self-discovery, healing, and transformation.

May these poems spark love deep inside,
May peace be with you, your constant guide.
May joy bloom in your solitary space,
May you find the strength to run life's race.

May you have the courage to show your true face,
May your inner power never be misplaced.
May greatness awake within your soul,
May your light and love, shine and console.

Velory Irungbam

Overcoming Limiting Beliefs

1. BREAKING FREE FROM THE CHAIN OF EXPECTATIONS

Why do we feel we always fall short?
Even when we give our all and pour our heart,
Deep down we still feel we're not enough,
Despite our painting, singing, dancing, and heartfelt stuff.

We strive for excellence, our best to show,
But why do we feel we don't measure up and glow?
Expectations from parents, teachers, and peers,
Their standards loom, causing us fears.

We chase after their benchmarks, trying to please,
But why do we ignore our own hearts and needs?
We're enough just as we are in the present moment,
No need to compare or feel inferior, to feel tormented.

Let's embrace ourselves with love and acceptance,
Not dwell on others' expectations, let go of that fence,
We are unique, with our own journey to pursue,
Let's celebrate ourselves, and our passions, for they are true.

2. THE NAGGING VOICE

There's a voice inside, I call her "Guardy",
Nagging and persistent, she's never tardy,
From the back of my mind, she comes creeping,
Telling me I'm not enough, never stopping or sleeping.

Not pretty, not smart, not intelligent, she drones,
Her words were a constant barrage of low tones,
Not generous, not lovable, not worthy, she reminds,
Leaving me feeling small, with shattered binds.

She pops in whenever I try to upgrade or advance,
Making me feel like I never had a chance,
But I know I'm more than her negative spiel,
My own worth and potential, her words cannot steal.

So, I'll show her the door, bid her adieu,
I'll prove her wrong and follow my heart true,
No more will I let her hold me down,
For I am enough, with my own unique crown.

3. FEAR OF FAILURE

What if I fall short of the mark?
What if my efforts were just a lark?
What if my plans hit a snag?
What if my work is a drag?

What if I disappoint those who expect?
What if my dreams seem to deflect?
What if my creations don't get applause?
What if I waste time on a lost cause?

What if fear creeps in when I'm alone?
What if it grips and me, makes me postpone?
What if it whispers, "don't even try"?
What if it feeds doubts, and makes me shy?

This fear of failure can hold me back,
Make me retreat, and lose track.
But now I see it for what it is:
A mirage of limits, a shadowed abyss.

So, I'll face it, with courage and might,
I'll show it my mettle, my inner light.
For what if I choose to believe,
That I'm enough, that I can achieve?

4. THE WOUND OF NOT GOOD ENOUGH

When I feel not good enough, it's hard to receive,
The love of others, my heart struggles to believe,
And I'm unable to give my own love in full,
My core wound, a weight that makes my heart feel dull.

In relationships, there's no thriving or health,
Assurance and safety order me, like elusive stealth,
Trust and acceptance seem just out of reach,
And compassion feels like a lesson hard to teach.

Disappointment is common, and feelings of being unlovable,
But it's a false mindset, from childhood, it's undeniable,
It's time to take charge, to rewrite this story I tell,
And heal from the core, to cherish every relationship well.

Let's heal this wound, and let love and acceptance in,
For when we feel good enough, true love can begin,
Let's rewrite our story and let go of the past,
To cherish each relationship, and make them last.

5. THE STRUGGLE TO OVERCOME THE NOT GOOD ENOUGH MINDSET

In the back of the mind, a voice that's haunting,
Keeps me in chains, my spirit daunting,
Expectations loom, a heavy weight to bear,
Stuck in place, too scared to dare.

A feeling of unworthiness, a constant numbness,
Love and acceptance, a distant hum,
Trust in self, a challenge unmet,
Disconnected from within, I am but a silhouette.

Relationships suffer, push and pull in vain,
Self-doubt grips, like a tightening chain,
Breaking free, an elusive dream,
Shining my light, a far-off gleam.

Rewriting the story, self-love to sow,
Overcoming the pain, to truly grow,
External validation, a fleeting mirage,
An antidote to freedom, found within, not in a barrage.

Embracing imperfection, vulnerability to own,
Uprooting the core wound, to finally feel known,
Healing and growth, a journey rough,
Yet worth it all, to come home to our authentic self, enough.

6. ANXIETY

Anxiety, oh anxiety,
You grip my heart and shake my mind,
With worries and fears so many,
Leaving me feeling so confined.

Why do you visit me, my friend?
Why do you make my heart race?
Am I falling sick, or is it an end?
Or is it something I cannot chase?

I wish I could overcome this fear,
And face the unknown with ease,
Though the journey ahead is not clear,
But I am ready to face it with keys.

Dear Fear, you're a protector I know,
But it's time for me to let go,
To take the next step and grow,
And face the challenges that show.

My heart and my head are at a war,
With conflicting thoughts and dreams,
But I choose to listen to my core,
And ignore the negative, or so it seems.

I'll face my fears and I'll be brave,
And I'll show the world what I can do,

For my passion and my heart, I'll pave,
And I'll make my dreams come true.

7. THE ROOTS OF "NOT GOOD ENOUGH"

The roots of "not good enough" go deep, they say,
And stem from places far beyond today,
From childhood wounds and limiting beliefs,
To norms of society and unattainable feats.

The tendrils of comparison and competition,
Feed the mindset, fuelling the condition,
And the fear of failure, rejection's sting,
Can take hold and make our hearts take the wing.

With negative self-talk, we perpetuate,
The cycle, deepening the roots' weight,
Past traumas and hurts, they too take part,
Shaping our sense of worth, and fracturing our heart.

External validation, we often seek,
To feel good enough, to find the peak,
But in the end, it's only self-awareness,
And self-compassion that bring forth awareness.

With growth and transformation, we can confront,
The roots, and overcome their hold, shunt,
The light inside, so bright and strong,
A new narrative, a beautiful song.

8. THE GAME OF SOCIAL MEDIA

The game of social media,
a constant source of comparison,
This leaves us chasing validation, caught in the illusion,
The highlights and filters, a distorted view,
Leaves us feeling inferior, unsure of what to do.

The pressure to present perfection, an endless quest,
Leads to self-doubt and insecurity, an unwelcome guest,
The endless scrolling, a bottomless pit,
Can cause mental anguish, bit by bit.

Our worth is reduced to likes and comments,
A false sense of worth, causing constant torment,
Advertisements telling us to buy and consume,
To fit in and belong, we become a mere costume.

The constant need to be productive and successful,
Can be draining, causing our spirit to be stressful,
Cyberbullying and online criticism, a painful sting,
Leaves us feeling unworthy, questioning everything.

To overcome the not good enough mindset, we must take a break,
Cultivate self-love, and heal for our own sake,
Disconnect from the noise, and reconnect with our heart,
That's where true worth lies, a beautiful work of art.

9. THE SENSATION OF INADEQUACY

The sensation of inadequacy,
Is akin to a fiery flame within me,
Stirring my gut,
Thrusting me down.

My body throbs,
My shoulders strain,
Demanding my focus,
Anxiety invading.

Each time I take action,
Say something,
Reveal myself to others,
Afraid of disapproval, my physique quivers.

My heart ignites,
My stomach churns,
I'm suffocating,
Gasping for air under this weight.

10. COMPARISON

Comparison is the nemesis of self-love,
The spark that kindles inadequacy's flame,
No matter what you achieve, it's never enough,
Diminishing you, belittling your name.

It shrinks you down, makes you feel so small,
Inferiority and poverty seep in,
A sense of lack permeates, it covers all,
A constant measuring against an imagined standard.

It's time to slay this foe, cut it off,
Take the reins, refuse to let it control,
The only comparison that matters is that of,
Who you once were, and how you've grown.

Look back at your progress, applaud how far you've come,
Not the distance of those who went before,
Your journey's yours, unique, and never done,
So, compare yourself to none, but progress evermore.

11. OVERCOMING SELF-DOUBT

My mind is heavy, my heart is sore,
With thoughts of failure, I can't ignore,
Am I good enough, will I succeed,
Or will I fall, like a defeated breed?

But I know deep down, these fears are just a mirage,
My doubts and anxieties, a mere garage,
It's time for me to face the unknown,
And leave behind the fears, I have grown.

I'll take a step, with courage and grace,
Embracing the challenge, with a smiling face,
I'll learn from failures, I'll rise above,
With every setback, I'll show my love.

For my passion and my dreams, they are real,
I'll not let self-doubt, make me feel,
I am worthy, I am enough,
With every step, I'll become tough.

So, I'll walk the path, with my head held high,
With confidence and belief, I'll touch the sky,
I'll overcome self-doubt, with grace and poise,
And live a life, filled with joys and noise.

12. DEAR PERFECTIONISM

Oh, my dear perfectionism,
What a burden, what a prison,
A never-ending quest for flawlessness,
Leaves me feeling helpless.

I keep climbing the ladder higher,
But happiness seems to expire,
For every milestone that I attain,
My joy is fleeting, and pain remains.

I can't celebrate or appreciate,
The victories that I accumulate,
My fear of losing what I've gained,
Leaves me feeling drained and restrained.

I'm afraid of attracting evil eyes,
And dimming others' shining skies,
Of not being good enough for the world,
Of my happiness being unfurled.

But this fear has caused me strife,
Holding back my true potential and life,
It's time to let go of perfectionism's reign,
And embrace all my flaws without any shame.

I'll accept you as you are, my dear perfectionism,
But I won't let you control my optimism,

I'll relish the goodness of my achievements,
And dance my way out of the fear and bereavements.

It's time to live without any regret,
To let go of the pain and the fret,
I'll embrace my imperfections with pride,
And let go of perfectionism, that's what I decide.

13. SELF-COMPASSION

Compassion blooms from deep within,
A cure for the pain we endure,
From feeling "not good enough" again,
Acceptance of self is the only true cure.

Only then can true compassion flow,
A balm to soothe and heal,
The very pain that seems to grow,
When self-judgment and doubt appeal.

Whether others accept us or not,
Appreciate, understand, or show compassion,
It's from within that we need to begot,
Real love, inspiration, and motivation.

For we alone are the source of healing,
In the midst of chaos, or pain,
We alone can foster inner feeling,
Of solace, growth, and self-love again.

2

Overcoming the Inner Critic through Poetry

1. MY INNER CRITIC

My inner critic, a voice ever-present,
Since childhood, its purpose was clear,
To protect me from harm, make me repent,
Correct mistakes, and sincerely steer.

Intentions pure, to guide and teach,
Accelerate growth and lead to a righteous path,
Yet as a child, those words did breach,
Making me feel "not enough," mere aftermath.

The voice that made me feel so small,
Belittling my worth, my true self unknown,
Belief in myself, a struggle above all,
Feeling good for nothing, all confidence has flown.

2. SILENCING THE INNER CRITIC

Oh, Inner Critic, dear friend, and foe,
Protector, nag, and voice of woe,
I long to silence you, yet also learn,
To manage your endless, ceaseless churn.

Are you not weary of causing me strife?
What do you seek to gain in life?
You make me feel small, never enough,
Never satisfied with what I accomplish.

Do you stem from my parents' voices?
Or societal standards with no good choices?
Expectations too high for a child's heart,
Leaving scars, tearing us apart.

We all bloom at different paces,
Each chapter brings its own traces,
So, let's not compare and strive,
But look to the past, and how we've survived.

Mother, I hear your voice so clear,
Father, I hear you too, my dear,
Teacher, Uncle, all those who teach,
Your intentions are pure, yet out of reach.

Perfectionism, an issue to dismiss,
Together, let's conquer and never miss,

The beauty in each mistake and flaw,
Let's embrace them all, and learn to soar.

3. IN THE STILLNESS

My rigid beliefs were questioned,
The anxiety of the unknown,
The anxiety of losing power,
The anxiety of rejection.

The anxiety of being alone,
The anxiety of causing harm,
Surged like ocean waves,
Overwhelmed by emotions.

Sinking in a sea of pain and misery,
I avoided these uneasy feelings,
By numbing or distracting myself,
But it only amplified the pain.

I was forced to confront these emotions,
Recognizing their need for attention,
Some stemming from past misconceptions,
Demanding my attention in stillness.

Only to find liberation,
By facing them head-on,
With full awareness,
Accepting them as they are.

Without judgment,
Without labels,

Without needing to express,
Just as they are.

In full awareness,
In full acceptance,
Creating space for freedom,
Creating space for love.

In stillness,
Nothing overpowers, but love prevails,
All along, this love was within me,
And this "me" was in the stillness, I once feared.

4. THE FEELING OF LETTING GO

Like a gust of wind that brushes through my skin,
I release the voice that nags within,
A wave of relief washes over me,
My body feels lighter, and my soul feels free.

As if a weight has been lifted from my chest,
I can finally breathe and take a moment of rest,
The knots in my gut begin to untangle,
My spirit is now free to soar and dangle.

5. POETRY, MY SAVING GRACE

Poetry has a gentle way to soothe,
The voice of Guardy, that barking dog so rude,
Who never leaves a stone unturned,
To remind me of all the ways I haven't learned.

But poetry is my saving grace,
A means to process and let go with grace,
Through verse, I find a way to release,
The nagging feeling and let it find peace.

Like a river that flows with ease,
My emotions now have room to breathe,
The words on the page are like a healing balm,
My spirit is now light, free from all harm.

6. EMBRACE AND RE-OWN YOURSELF

Oh, dear not good enough, self-doubt and fear,
Comparison and procrastination, jealousy so near,
From where do you come, to make me feel so low,
With each step you take, my confidence does slow.

I wish to run and hide, beneath the earth's crack,
But where can I flee, to escape your attack,
I long to settle this feud, and make you depart,
For your presence leaves me feeling weak in heart.

Experts say you're a part of me, that I've disowned,
Suppressed and repressed, for years I've atoned,
But now you appear through others, a mirror to my past,
A reminder that the feelings I've kept locked, still last.

So let us sit and talk, face to face and heart to heart,
Tell me who you are, and why you've played this part,
Are you here to harm, or to help me evolve,
For I've been taught, to not feel and to absolve.

Now I know, acceptance is the key, to re-owning a part,
Denial only adds, to the pain in my heart,
So let us embrace, and no longer be strangers,
For together we'll find peace, and rid of all dangers.

7. I AM ENOUGH

I am enough, no matter what they say,
I was born perfectly whole in every way,
No need for approval or validation,
I am complete, without hesitation.

My past beliefs may have held me back,
But now I see, it was just an attack,
On my self-worth and inner truth,
But I am enough, that's my proof.

The core wound, those plagued us all,
Is the belief that we will fall,
Short of some ideal standard,
But I am enough, that is the answer.

All wars could end if we just knew,
That we are enough, through and through,
No need to chase fame, money, or power,
I am enough, that's my shining tower.

No longer will I hide behind a wall,
To protect me from any fall,
I will step out and embrace my truth,
I am enough, that's my breakthrough.

It's time to rewrite the story I tell,
To let go of the beliefs that held me in hell,

I am enough, and that's all that matters,
My inner light shines, and my soul never shatters.

So, I am here feeling so excited,
To write a poem on how to be ignited,
To let go of the belief of not enough,
To embrace the truth that we are already tough.

8. GIVE YOURSELF THE LOVE

In words that are gentle and kind,
Show compassion to yourself in mind,
As you would do for others in strife,
When they are struggling in their life.

In the midst of a battle of head and heart,
Acceptance is where the war can depart,
When the voices in conflict, can't agree,
Self-compassion can bring harmony.

I know it's not simple, it takes time,
But take a step and see the climb,
Of the ease with which you'll find peace,
By giving yourself, love and release.

9. A DIALOGUE WITH FEAR

"Why do you haunt me, Fear?" I ask,
"Why do you make my life a task?"
"I am here to protect," it replies,
"To keep you safe, to not fall and rise."

Fear, why do you haunt my every thought,
Making me question what I have wrought,
Is it a sign of impending doom,
Or just my mind playing this game of gloom?

I feel dizzy and lost, my heart races,
With every thought of the future and unknown places,
Is it a sign that I am not good enough,
Or are just my doubts putting up a tough?

But I know deep down, I must face you,
To overcome the fear, I must get through,
I am ready to face whatever lies ahead,
With courage and faith, I'll stand up from the bed.

Dear Fear, I know you mean well,
But it's time for me to break free from this cell,
I'll make mistakes, I'll stumble and fall,
But I'll pick myself up, standing tall.

So, Fear, let's have a dialogue today,
I'll listen to you; you listen to what I say,

I am ready to face the world, with a brave heart,
With courage, I'll take a step, a brand-new start.

10. THE SWEETEST JOY OF BREAKING FREE

No happiness can measure up,
To break free from chains that corrupt,
Illusions that held us down,
Now shattered and no longer around.

No liberation can be compared,
To sever cords that never cared,
For our growth or our delight,
No longer do we have to fight.

No enjoyment can ever be,
As sweet as when we finally see,
Our inner conflicts meet their end,
No more turmoil that we must fend.

3

Learning to Love Your Imperfections

1. LEARNING TO CELEBRATE IMPERFECTIONS

I embrace who I am,
All my goodness, flaws, and sham.
Imperfect, yet I celebrate,
Mistakes too, I celebrate.

In the past, I sought perfection,
Hiding messy parts with deception.
Showing only the best of me,
Hiding the rest, oh so secretly.

Under the rug, I kept them all,
Unseen, unheard, in a hidden haul.
Even from myself, I concealed,
The parts I feared, and never revealed.

Unknowingly, they surfaced through,
Projections of others, my clue.
Surprised, I wondered how,
Those parts I hid, surfaced now?

I realized then, it was time to embrace,
And celebrate each part with grace.
For these parts, though hidden and suppressed,
Were still a part of me, and deserved to be expressed.

Celebrating them, brought me peace,
And helped me see a new release.
Now, I accept them in me and in others,
For embracing imperfections, liberates us like no other.

2. I CELEBRATE EVERY PART OF ME

I celebrate every part of me, unique and true,
Embracing imperfections, flaws and all that's due,
I don't hide behind a mask, but let my true self shine,
For who I am is whom I love, and that's just fine.

I celebrate my quirks, the things that make me,
My loud voice, my body's shape, and my teeth that are misaligned with glee,
For it's in these imperfections, that I find my strength,
And learn to live a life, where self-love takes the reins.

I celebrate my mistakes, the times when things go wrong,
For they help me learn, grow, and sing a different song,
I celebrate the days when I feel down and blue,
For even in the darkness, light can still come through.

I celebrate the parts of me, that some may call boring,
For it's in these moments, that I find a peaceful soaring,
And when I'm feeling stubborn, and refuse to change my ways,
I learn to let go and embrace the joy of new days.

So let us all celebrate, each imperfection that we bear,
For it's in these very things, that make us oh so rare,
And when we love ourselves, just as we are and ought to be,
We open up our hearts, to a life full of harmony.

3. IMPERFECTIONS ADD BEAUTY

Imperfections add beauty, they add depth,
Like the brush strokes on a canvas, they create a unique concept.
They're like the clouds that adorn the sky,
Or the scar that adds beauty to the moon up high.

Each imperfection is a piece of the mosaic,
That forms a beautiful picture of our personaic.
They're like the veins in a leaf so fine,
Adding texture and interest to the design.

Just like a diamond, each imperfection,
Can make us more valuable with distinction.
Like the crooked branches of a tree so tall,
They add character and uniqueness to us all.

Imperfections are like grains in a piece of wood,
Making us stand out and be understood.
Like the rust on old metal, they bring beauty to the fore,
Adding depth to our lives and making us shine more.

Each imperfection is like a star in the night sky,
Adding to the wonder and beauty of our lives that pass by.
Like the crevices in a mountain so grand,
They make us more interesting and help us stand.

Imperfections add beauty, they add depth,
Each one adds character and makes it unique with a concept.

Like a beautiful melody, imperfections add harmony,
Enriching our lives and making us a masterpiece, undoubtedly.

4. IMPERFECTIONS MAKE US HUMAN

We rise, we fall like waves in the sea,
Life's lessons, and mistakes, shape you and me.
But fear of failure can keep us stuck in place,
Afraid to stumble and fall on our face.

As a child, we're taught to avoid all mistakes,
But that mindset is flawed, it's what's at stake.
Without taking chances and trying new things,
We'll never know what life's adventure brings.

Think back to when we learned how to walk,
Each wobbly step, was a victory to talk.
And learning to ride a bike, with each fall,
We gained the strength to ride like a pro and stand tall.

The road to success is paved with imperfect tries,
The journey is where the beauty lies.
Champions aren't made without any flaws,
It's the imperfections that give depth and cause.

So don't be afraid of making mistakes,
Embrace them as chances to learn and take.
For it's through the flaws that we grow and thrive,
Our humanity and our imperfections make us come alive.

5. LOVING MY FLAWS

Loving my flaws was not an easy feat,
A battle within, an exhausting defeat,
But I learned to surrender, to let go,
To embrace every flaw, to let it show.

Like the universe's gentle embrace,
My flaws held beauty, a different grace,
Disowned parts of me found acceptance,
The universe's lesson, a welcome presence.

People came and loved what I tried to hide,
I felt safe, no longer had to subside,
I realized I'm responsible to love every part,
To show up as is, to love with an open heart.

Nature taught me to love myself as I am,
To embrace each flaw, like a precious gem,
As above, so below, those words I now know,
Rediscovering myself, my beauty starts to glow.

6. THE PROCESS OF EMBRACING IMPERFECTIONS

Like a garden of diverse flowers,
each with its own unique hue,
Like a symphony of different notes, creating something new,
Like a puzzle with pieces of all shapes and sizes,
Embracing imperfections can be like a journey of surprises.

It takes courage to face our flaws and see them for what they are,
To accept and love ourselves, including the parts that may leave a scar,
It takes patience to navigate the twists and turns along the way,
To trust the process and believe that imperfections will lead us to a
brighter day.

Resilience is needed when we stumble or fall,
To pick ourselves up and keep moving, despite it all,
Letting go of what no longer serves us, like leaves falling from a tree,
Clearing the way for growth and new possibilities to see.

Love for self and others is the foundation on which we build,
A place of compassion, kindness, and acceptance, where we are fulfilled,
Embracing imperfections may not always be easy or fun,
But it can lead us to a life where we shine brighter than the sun.

7. IMPERFECTIONS AS SOURCES OF STRENGTH

Our imperfections, like stepping stones,
Guide us through life's winding roads,
They may seem small, but each one,
Adds to the story that makes us whole.

Our imperfections are the reasons,
We're able to laugh and smile today,
For they're the building blocks that pave,
The path to a brighter, better way.

Like the stones that make up a riverbed,
Our imperfections form the foundation,
That allows us to stand strong and brave,
Through any obstacle or situation.

And though they may seem small and flawed,
Each imperfection adds a unique touch,
A chapter in the book of our lives,
That makes us who we are, as such.

8. THE FEELING OF ACCEPTING AND LOVING YOUR IMPERFECTIONS

It's an incredible feeling to soar like an eagle, free and unchained,
To embrace and cherish all my imperfections unashamed,
My body moves with fluidity and grace, unencumbered and unburdened,
My heart beats with a newfound rhythm, a melody I've learned.

My shoulders relax and my breathing slows as if a weight has been lifted,
A sense of warmth and peace spreads through me as if my soul has been gifted.
The gentle touch of self-love, like a warm embrace from a loved one,
A deep exhale of relief, like a journey that's finally done.

The taste of honey on my lips, like a sweetness that I savor,
The melody of my voice is like a song that I can savor.
A clarity of mind, like a fog that has lifted to reveal,
The beauty of my true self, that I can now finally feel.

The sight of a sunset, like a canvas that's painted in hues,
A sense of belonging and connection, like a feeling that I cannot refuse.
The fragrance of a blooming rose, like a perfume that fills the air,
A sense of contentment and joy, like a heart that's without care.

9. VULNERABILITY AND SELF-ACCEPTANCE

Vulnerability is not a weakness,
but a strength to behold,
To be open about flaws and imperfections, to be bold.
Self-acceptance is to embrace all parts, even those we fear,
To deny or hide our perceived weaknesses is not the answer.

The fear of being vulnerable can hold us back,
Preventing us from accepting ourselves and the world's track.
But if we embrace vulnerability, we'll gain insight,
Understanding ourselves and others, with newfound might.

Empathy and connection are fostered by vulnerability,
Helping us to accept ourselves and others, building camaraderie.
Self-acceptance leads to resilience and taking risks,
Living in alignment with values, not societal tricks.

Vulnerability is a catalyst for growth and development,
Confronting fears and limitations, facing our impediment.
Self-compassion arises from self-acceptance and vulnerability,
Kindness and understanding replace criticism and hostility.

The connection between vulnerability and self-acceptance,
Creates a healthy and fulfilling sense of self, a new stance.
For accepting our vulnerabilities and flaws,
Allows us to live a life without pause.

10. FREEDOM OF EMBRACING IMPERFECTIONS

Embracing imperfections, a path to liberation,
Break free from others' standards, a heart's palpitation.
No need to prove oneself or bear the shame,
For not measuring up to society's game.

Validation and approval, are no longer sought,
Perfectionism's burden, from you, is caught.
Flaws become features that add to your grace,
True self shines through, without fear or disgrace.

Freedom of self-acceptance, an unparalleled thrill,
As a caged bird is freed, it soars with a will.
With no weight of judgment, you fly high,
Embracing imperfections, with wings you can touch the sky.

11. SELF-LOVE AND SELF-ACCEPTANCE

Self-love is the foundation for a life that's fulfilling,
Accepting imperfections, to grow it's thrilling.
Comparison to others leads to self-doubt and despair,
Criticizing ourselves, only leaves us in despair.

Embracing our imperfections can bring self-confidence,
Understanding and accepting, flaws with all deference.
We're all imperfect, unique in every way,
Self-love enables us, to love others come what may.

By embracing our flaws, we can overcome our fears,
Limiting beliefs, dissolve in self-love's tears.
Self-acceptance is the key, to happiness and joy,
No need to seek perfection, let that feeling of inadequacy destroy.

Self-love is the antidote, to life that's unfulfilled,
Self-acceptance is the key, to a life that's thrilled.
Strength amidst uncertainty, from self-love we derive,
Amidst challenges, self-acceptance helps us thrive.

We're responsible for our own love, that's true,
Accepting all our flaws, that's love overdue.
Safe room for mistakes, self-love creates,
Accepting others' mistakes, self-acceptance demonstrates.

Harmony and health, in relationships we see,
Embracing differences, with more love and empathy.

Self-love and acceptance, the foundation of all,
A better world, where love and kindness stand tall.

4

Finding Self-Acceptance through Poetry

1. THE JOURNEY TO SELF-ACCEPTANCE

When I first embarked on my quest
to know who I am,
I struggled to embrace parts of me that others deemed a sham.
Caregivers, society, and the environment all had their say,
I hid my true self away, pretending to be okay.

Like a balloon submerged in water, it kept floating up,
Revealing itself, demanding to be seen, refusing to be stuck.
But I resisted, denied, and judged both myself and others,
Playing the game of disassociation, hurting sisters and brothers.

Then came a turning point, a trigger-fueled evolution,
I realized that to heal, I needed awareness and re-owning of my contribution.
Slowly but surely, I started to accept each part of me,
And with self-acceptance, came a natural flow of empathy.

Compassion for self and others, a balm for all our wounds,
As everything falls into place, love abounds.
No longer hiding, pretending, or numbing parts of me,
I am free to be me, accepting and loving, unconditionally.

2. THE POWER OF POETRY IN UNCOVERING SELF-ACCEPTANCE

In the art of poetry, I find freedom unbound,
A therapy that acknowledges triggers, and emotions unshackled, ungrounded.
A channel to express my innermost thoughts and feelings,
To feel seen, heard, and acknowledged, my identity revealing.

Poetry connects me with diverse souls from every place,
Helps me release all suppressed emotions with ease and grace.
It helps me reflect, understand myself, and gain clarity,
Finding solutions to life's challenges is an artistic rarity.

A great antidepressant and painkiller, poetry is a cure,
Soothing my heart, giving rest to my body, gentle and pure.
It enhances my creativity, igniting my imagination,
Connecting me to my body and all elements, a beautiful sensation.

In my flaws and imperfections, poetry helps me find beauty,
Questioning societal norms, creating awareness, a poetic duty.
Connecting with kindred spirits, on journeys of self-acceptance,
Making peace with the inner war, reconciling heart and conscience.

With clarity of mind, making better decisions, and finding ease,
Poetry's been a balm for embracing total self-acceptance with grace and breeze.

It's a tool for empowerment, growth, and transformation,
Opening up new possibilities, with each line's formation.

3. DISCOVERING THE INNER BEAUTY

Within us lies a beauty, so vast and deep,
That can only be unlocked by the self-love we keep.
When we commit to caring for ourselves every day,
Reflections and introspection lead us to find our way.

It's our responsibility to nurture and tend,
To the parts of ourselves, we've neglected and penned.
By taking ownership of our lives, we can change
The way we relate to ourselves and all those in range.

Embracing our imperfections, we become flawlessly unique,
Forgiveness flows easily and is transformative and meek.
We face the pain, let go of hurts, and move on,
Finding beauty and purpose, in the battles, we have won.

Mindfulness and inner peace we begin to seek,
Gratitude and appreciation flow naturally in our creek.
Connecting with nature and the world around,
We find joy and inner beauty that was previously unfound.

4. BREAKING FREE FROM SELF-JUDGMENT

In the past, I used to constantly critique myself,
From my every action to my every word on the shelf.
I judged myself as not good enough, not smart enough, not pretty
enough,
And these thoughts kept me stuck, never feeling tough.

Even when I received recognition, I couldn't trust,
I believed it was just luck, and not because I must
Have been good enough to deserve it in the end,
My self-criticism never ceased, always around the bend.

It wasn't until my body broke down in pain,
That I realized this judgement was causing me strain.
I had to find a way to heal, to break the cycle,
To understand where it came from, to reconcile.

I sat with my emotions, triggers, and pain,
And finally began to embrace and acknowledge the strain.
Slowly, I started to connect with myself again,
And breaking free from self-judgment wasn't such a strain.

Weighed down by self-judgment, our souls become heavy,
Hindered by insecurities, never finding levity.
But we can challenge these thoughts, and see ourselves anew,
Embracing our unique beauty, and all that we can do.

By cultivating self-compassion, and treating ourselves with care,
We can challenge the limiting beliefs we hold and let go of the despair.
Mistakes and failures are a part of growth, a chance to learn and try,
With self-love and acceptance, we can soar and reach the sky.

So let us break free from the shackles of self-judgment and shame,
Embracing our unique selves and all that makes us one of a kind, never
tame.
Let us step into our power, our light shining bright,
And love ourselves fiercely, with all our might.

5. THE HEALING MAGIC OF WORDS

The potency of words is undeniable,
They can uplift us or leave us unstable.
They hold the power to shape our fate,
And determine if we'll love or hate.

Yet, when spoken with purpose and care,
They can help us heal and become aware.
The magic of words lies in their ability,
To transform our reality with ease and agility.

They can help us release the past and move on,
And provide us with the strength to carry on.
Words can be used to build or destroy,
But let's choose to use them as a tool of joy.

Let's speak with kindness and not with spite,
And in doing so, let's spread love and light.
For the healing magic of words is true,
And can bring us hope and renew.

Let's harness their power to create a better world,
Where love, kindness, and compassion are unfurled.
Let's choose our words to uplift and inspire,
And use them to create a world that's higher.

6. THE COURAGE TO LOVE YOURSELF

Loving oneself can be daunting and tough,
In a world that often says, "You're not enough."
It takes courage to ignore the outside noise,
And instead, focus on one's own inner voice.

To prioritize self-care, and not feel guilty,
To invest in oneself, and feel more worthy.
To cultivate self-love, and let it grow,
To let oneself flourish, and let oneself glow.

It takes courage to believe in oneself,
To trust one's abilities, and not feel helpless.
To see one's potential, and pursue it with zeal,
To stay focused on the goal, and not let fear steal.

Loving oneself takes a lot of work,
But the rewards are worth it, and the journey can perk.
For when we love ourselves, we attract love and light,
And we become a beacon, shining bright.

7. REWRITING THE NARRATIVE

We all create stories to define who we are,
We learn from others, near and far.
Repetitive words give us meaning,
And shape our thoughts with each repeating.

The stories we hear become our own,
We carry them forward, and they are shown.
We search for evidence to prove our tale,
And sometimes forget we can rewrite and prevail.

We hold the power to change the narrative,
To edit and rewrite what we believe.
With pen in hand, we can make a new start,
And change the story that once broke our heart.

Life can be filled with struggles and pain,
But a positive shift can ease the strain.
Finding the lessons in the midst of strife,
And embracing gratitude in every part of life.

Rewriting our narrative means facing our fears,
Believing in ourselves, and shedding our tears.
It's about taking chances and expanding our mind,
And embracing the unknown, leaving our fears behind.

So let us take control of our own fate,
And write a story that feels truly great.

A tale of hope, resilience, and growth,
A story that reflects the best of both.

8. THE LIBERATION OF SELF-ACCEPTANCE

When we begin to accept ourselves for who we are,
We cultivate a stronger bond that takes us far.
No longer burdened by expectations or guilt,
We release the weight of shame and the regrets we've built.

With each step forward, we feel calmer and lighter,
Able to give ourselves permission to make mistakes and grow brighter.
We hold space for all emotions, even the uncomfortable kind,
Developing compassion for ourselves, with a newfound peace of mind.

We breathe easier, handle stress better, and walk in freedom,
Living in the present, and relishing each moment with wisdom.
We become conscious of the beauty that surrounds us,
Gratitude comes easier, and life becomes simpler without fuss.

We find joy in our own company, and in others we meet,
Embracing our flaws and uniqueness, shining bright and sweet.
The liberation of self-acceptance is a journey worth taking,
A journey of forgiveness, love, and power in the making.

So let us break free from the chains that have held us down,
And find the freedom and joy of self-love that abounds.
Let us embrace the beauty of our humanity, with all its complexities,
And find peace and serenity, like waves on the sea, with ease.

9. EMBRACING ALL OF YOU

You are more than just a body, mind,
thoughts, or emotions.
You're not just defined by success or failures or any titles or labels.
There's much more to you than meets the eye, and even beyond perception.
You're not just limited to the conscious or the outward expression.

You have all emotions, good and bad,
And different personalities,
Some you're aware of and some you're not.
You're not only what you say or do, but also what you don't.

You are everything - the forms and the formlessness,
the concepts and beyond concepts,
the conscious and the unconscious.
You're one with all.

Embracing yourself means embracing all of it.
Embracing all of your goodness, flaws, and imperfections.
Embracing all of your stories, mistakes, past, present, and future.
You are whole, within, and without.

Let go of the pain and scars, and love every part of yourself,
Including those that feel broken or unspoken.
Accept your flaws, vulnerabilities, and imperfections,
And find your voice, celebrating your uniqueness.

Live in the present, recognize the light that shines inside,
And embrace your true self without any fear or shame.
Embrace every part of who you are, with love and care,
And celebrate the beauty of your uniqueness, shining like a guiding star.

10. THE JOURNEY HOME

The path we walk is not a straight line,
Full of ups and downs that we will find.
Sometimes the way is hard to see,
And we may feel lost and far from free.

But there are times when we feel inspired,
And we keep going even when we're tired.
We face sickness, failure, and doubt,
But we keep pushing until we figure it out.

There are times when we think we're there,
And other times when it seems so rare.
We lose trust in ourselves and others too,
And forget the love that we once knew.

We blame ourselves and those around,
For losing the way and not being found.
But every part of the journey has a purpose,
And with time, we'll learn to embrace and harness.

We'll realize that the road leads to acceptance and love,
And that we are capable of rising above.
It's not just about reaching a place,
But finding ourselves and our true face.

We learn to love and accept who we are,
And to shine like the brightest star.
We find peace and release on this path,
And live with purpose, joy, and a good laugh.

So let us embrace this journey that we roam,
And trust that we will find our way home.
For the road we travel may not be straight,
But with each step, we grow and create.

5

Celebrating Self-Love and Empowerment

1. THE JOURNEY TO SELF-LOVE

My path to self-love began,
When I felt stuck in the mud and quicksand,
When my mind was a blank slate,
And I had to release my titles and labels, and accept my fate.

I lost my sense of self,
In the pursuit of external wealth.
I was facing an existential crisis,
And filled my mind with questions and vices.

Who am I and what's my purpose?
Why am I here, is it all worth it?
I joined personal development courses,
And met friends and teachers who were my forces.

I learned many modalities,
And faced many harsh realities.
Some people left and rejected me,
But they taught me the lesson of self-love ultimately.

At first, I was searching for love outside,
Blaming and shaming others, and feeling denied.
I was angry, demanding attention from my loved ones,
Not understanding why they couldn't meet my wants and needs, my
stunned.

I didn't know why they couldn't love me the way I wanted,
Or why they chose to abandon me, feeling daunted.
I gave my all, only to feel not enough,
Living in insecurity and fear, it was rough.

My body finally gave me a call,
To listen and attend to my needs, to heal it all.
Friends like Angels came to rescue me,
To help me find myself and love me, finally free.

Songs, movies, and nature all reminded me to look within,
And slowly but surely, I began to begin.
Picking up the pieces, gathering my soul fragments,
I finally found the answers to my whys, with no judgments.

I fell in love with myself all over again,
Feeling fulfilled from within.
All my unmet needs began meeting,
I rescued myself and found who I was seeking.

This is the story of my journey to self-love,
It wasn't easy, but it was worth every shove.
Now it's your turn, tell me your tale,
Of how you found your self-love, and how you did prevail

2. THE POWER OF POETRY IN CULTIVATING SELF-LOVE

I began with self-expression,
Writing in my journal without hesitation.
At first, it was just leisure,
But soon became a healing treasure.

As I challenged myself to find the right words,
I discovered poetry's power to release all my hurts.
With creativity or straightforward expression,
I found my emotions and found some resolution.

Poetry became my companion,
A tool to help me find self-love,
As I felt heard and understood,
Connected to others in a way that's good.

Through poetry, I could rediscover myself,
My voice, my heart, my inner wealth.
And so, I share this gift with you,
Poetry can heal us too.

3. UNLEASHING YOUR INNER POWER

Embrace all of you, to unlock your inner power so true,
Acknowledge all feelings, let them guide you through,
Be authentic, be one with your Higher Self,
Commit to healing, and put your own needs on the shelf.

Give yourself love, be the parent you always wanted,
Speak up for yourself, let your voice be undaunted,
Detach from seeking validation and approval,
Make self-care and self-love your daily renewal.

Trust your inner guidance, surround yourself with the uplifting few,
Take consistent, imperfect action towards your dream anew,
Through setbacks, let resilience be your guide,
Keep loving yourself, and let self-love reside.

Unlock your inner power, it's always been inside.
It may take some time to find, but don't let that deter,
Through the challenges and struggles, your inner power will stir,
Believe in your own strength, and your potential will occur.

4. THE TRIUMPH OF SELF-LOVE

Self-love brings triumph, it's true,
The more you prioritize it, the more you renew,
Committing to your own healing, and stepping outside your zone,
Brings happiness and excitement, and helps you to be known.

Get to know yourself, stand up for what you believe,
Show up as your authentic self, and you will achieve,
The power and responsibility to work on yourself, you'll find,
Embracing all parts of you, and leaving what's not kind,
Integrating your true self, and letting go of what's not true,
This is the ultimate triumph of self-love, for me and you.

5. EMBRACING YOUR STRENGTH

Discover your strengths, both big and small,
Use them to tackle weaknesses and stand tall,
Through resilience, we can achieve our best,
By persisting, we unlock treasures to manifest.

Empowering ourselves with self-love,
Gives us the courage to keep going above,
Letting go of the lie that we're not enough,
Takes strength, but it's worth it, that's the stuff.

Embrace all our flaws and imperfections,
Let go of false narratives, make corrections,
Write new stories that align with who we are,
Feel all our feelings, be our own guiding star.

Through inner reflection and introspection,
We know ourselves better, our true reflection,
Healing ourselves takes time, even if we can't see,
But with consistency and resilience, we can set ourselves free.

So, my dear friend, let's embrace our strength,
Fall in love with ourselves, go to great length,
To live life fully, with self-love as our guide,
And let our inner light shine, with nothing to hide.

6. THE TRANSFORMATIVE MAGIC OF SELF-LOVE

Self-love is Magic, it's pure and true,
Transforming all that's old and renewing you,
The antidote to healing, it mends the soul,
Making your heart's desires your life's goal.

With self-love, new doors will open wide,
Opportunities abound, the world is your guide,
You'll find the courage to follow your heart,
And be your true self, a brand-new start.

No guilt or shame, just liberty,
A weight lifted off, you can finally be,
Self-love will boost your career and create wealth,
Bringing the right relationships and harmony, good health.

Self-love gives us the strength to face life's challenges,
And show up as our authentic selves, with no more imbalances,
More peace and fulfillment, in and around,
Compassion and being present, a life newly found.

Procrastination is gone, mindset upgraded,
Compassion and abundance, love unabated,
It can change your entire reality, it's true,
The transformative magic of self-love, in all that you do.

7. BREAKING FREE FROM LIMITATIONS

Our minds can hold us back, that's true,
With limiting beliefs, we can't push through,
Our impressions and past weigh us down,
Like invisible chains that leave us bound.

But we can break free and find our way,
To a brighter future, a brand-new day,
We can shatter beliefs that don't serve,
And from our old patterns, we can swerve.

Let go of ancestral tales,
That doesn't support us, and often fail,
The pressures of society and culture,
We can discard and not let them torture.

We must choose to think on our own,
And not just follow the path that's shown,
We can find our own truth and light,
And let go of illusions, day or night.

We can shift our mindset from scarcity,
To one of abundance and prosperity,
With love, success, and beauty redefined,
Breaking free, we can be aligned.

So, let's break free from limitations,
And open up to new creations,

Embrace ourselves, and all we can be,
And live our lives authentically free.

8. UNLEASHING YOUR LIGHT

Choosing self-love unlocks a door,
To prioritize what is healthy and good for,
Self-care becomes your daily chore,
For your mental and emotional core.

You start making choices that uplift,
Your own welfare, your own gift,
Discovering values, making a shift,
To align with your own spirit.

With each choice, you gain might,
Unleashing your power, shining bright,
Becoming your highest version in sight,
Living fulfilled and taking flight.

Self-love unlocks this hidden gem,
The power within you, to the brim,
Shedding any doubts, let your light beam,
Self-love is the key, let it gleam.

9. EMBRACING YOUR INNER WARRIOR

Embrace your inner warrior, it takes courage,
But once you do, you'll feel the surge,
Embrace your inner warrior, it takes strength,
But it's worth it to go to any length.

With self-love comes a newfound power,
To bring out the best and never cower,
Embracing imperfections and flaws,
Unleashes the warrior's fierce claws.

With this power, you'll cut away,
Whatever no longer serves you in any way,
Empowered to be your true self,
Free from fear of rejection and the need to prove oneself.

No need for validation or recognition,
As you embody your own true mission,
And when things don't go as planned,
Your inner warrior will take a stand.

Fighting through any fire and storm,
As you know the power within, it's not just a norm,
It's time to release the chains you've placed,
And embrace the warrior you've always faced.

10. TRANSCENDING

Transcending the feeling of not being good enough,
Transcending the fear of rejection's rough,
Transcending the pressure of societal norms,
Transcending the beliefs that kept me in forms.

Transcending the need for perfection's embrace,
Transcending the approval, I once chased,
Transcending the craving to be understood,
Transcending the love sought from beyond my hood.

Transcending the hunger for attention's call,
Transcending the constant need to prove my worth to all,
Transcending the need for external validation,
Transcending the desire for acceptance and admiration.

Transcending the need to be seen and heard,
Transcending the need to be always right, the need to be spurred,
Transcending the need to stand out from the crowd,
Transcending the need to be the best that's loud.

Transcending all these needs and more,
The person who meets all my needs is right at my core,
Realizing at last, I was searching for myself in others,
True happiness and love come from within and are discovered by self-discovery's covers.

6

Navigating Relationships with Self-Love and Confidence

1. THE ART OF SELF-LOVE IN RELATIONSHIPS

To form a bond with others that's pure.
You must create one with yourself, for sure.
Self-love can feel selfish at first,
And guilty too, as though your heart may burst.

Change is scary, and fear is real,
We worry that others won't stick and will reveal,
That we don't belong, we don't fit in,
But choosing ourselves is how love begins.

It's terrifying when love falls apart,
When the person we cherish breaks our heart,
But choosing to love ourselves is the key,
To find the love we've been searching to see.

No love is like the one we can give,
To ourselves, that's the only way to truly live,
The emptiness we try to fill with others,
Can only be filled by loving ourselves, our true lovers.

Self-love is an art, it takes time,
To embrace our imperfections, the flaws we find,
To accept ourselves, forgive, and be grateful too,
To work through our triggers, and let go when we're through.

Loving ourselves, even on a hard day,
Breaking patterns, keeping hope when there seems no way,
Fake it until you make it, and it becomes natural,
An art with all shades of emotions, it's beautiful.

Self-love is an art, and we are the creator
It's a lifelong process, but we'll be greater.
With each day we grow stronger and wiser,
As we continue to love and prioritize ourselves, our own advisor.

2. THE POWER OF POETRY IN NAVIGATING RELATIONSHIPS WITH CONFIDENCE

The power of poetry helps navigate
relationships with confidence,
It unleashes all feelings and helps you make sense.
Through poetry, you can express and release emotions,
And find the freedom to be your true self without commotions.

Poetry fulfills the need to be heard and seen,
It beautifies the mind and brings clarity to things.
It adds joy, playfulness, and a sense of fun,
And helps you prepare for tough conversations to come.

Poetry helps you see the good in yourself and others,
And portrays it all with beautiful metaphors.
It helps you navigate relationships with ease,
And boosts your confidence to be who you want to be.

Poetry is a powerful tool for communication,
It brings people together in harmony and cohesion.
It helps you navigate any relationship with grace,
And helps you find your inner peace in any case.

3. SELF-LOVE IN RELATIONSHIPS

Self-love is the foundation of any relationship's strength,
It allows for growth and intimacy of great length,
It opens up the doors to compassion and understanding,
And leads to a love that is truly outstanding.

When we love ourselves, we attract those who see our worth,
And together, we can create a bond that will give birth,
To a love that is fulfilling and true,
With a foundation of self-love to guide us through.

Self-love in relationships means being kind and gentle,
Not just to our partners, but also to ourselves, it's essential,
It means embracing imperfections and learning from mistakes,
And creating a safe space for vulnerability to take place.

So let us start with loving ourselves first,
And let our love for others grow and burst,
With a foundation of self-love that is strong and true,
We can navigate relationships with confidence and see them through.

4. THE JOY OF BOUNDLESS SELF-LOVE IN RELATIONSHIPS

When boundless self-love is in play,
Our relationships bloom in a beautiful way,
We're free from the fear of rejection,
And our hearts can feel the pure connection.

Joy fills our hearts, no need to please,
We love ourselves, with all our needs,
We radiate love from deep within,
And our relationships become a win-win.

Our authenticity shines so bright,
And attracts others with its light,
We embrace our flaws, imperfections and all,
And our relationships stand tall.

With boundless self-love as our guide,
Our relationships blossom and thrive,
We create a loving, harmonious space,
Where joy and love take center place.

5. NAVIGATING RELATIONSHIPS WITH CONFIDENCE

When navigating relationships with confidence,
Self-love is the key to your inner brilliance,
It breaks insecurities and fears' fence,
And builds trust with genuine allegiance.

It gives you the courage to speak your mind,
And set healthy boundaries that are aligned,
To be yourself, no need to hide behind,
And have deep conversations that you find.

Through self-love, you find meaning in relation,
And patience to hold space with affection,
You love from your deepest soul's sensation,
And have the confidence to face any situation.

You know your worth and what you bring,
And cherish the good moments that you sing,
With full confidence, you navigate and wing,
Deep connections and good memories you bring.

6. THE FREEDOM OF SELF-LOVE

Self-love brings freedom, that much is clear,
Freedom to be yourself without any fear,
Express yourself fully, make decisions with ease,
Live by your rules and follow your inner breeze.

Your authenticity shines when you love yourself first,
Being true to your words, not quenching your thirst,
Follow your dreams and share them with pride,
Don't aim for perfection, just let yourself ride.

Don't compare yourself to others, let go of that measure,
Love without expectations, and be a joyous treasure,
Self-love brings freedom, from burden and stress,
Embrace it fully, and let yourself progress.

7. THE BALANCE OF SELF-LOVE AND CONNECTION

The balance of self-love and connection is key,
It helps you know your worth and set boundaries with glee.
You can give and receive love with ease,
And have deep connections that bring you peace.

You honor your needs and desires,
And also respect those of others without any fires.
You prioritize self-love and connection with care,
And find a balance that's unique and fair.

8. THE BEAUTY OF SELF-LOVE IN VULNERABILITY

When you let your walls down,
you're a sight to behold,
When you speak your truth, your beauty is gold,
Your flaws and imperfections, make you unique,
In vulnerability, your beauty peaks.

Opening up and expressing your heart,
Is a thing of beauty, a true work of art,
Letting go of proving your worth,
Adds to your beauty, a sense of mirth.

Honesty with yourself and others is rare,
It adds to your beauty, so take a dare,
To show your vulnerabilities is not a flaw,
It's a way to show the beauty of who you are.

In loving yourself and others with authenticity,
You radiate beauty, full of positivity,
Self-acceptance and standing up for yourself,
Adds to your beauty, like a shining elf.

Falling and making mistakes are human,
It's okay to show your emotions, to be a true woman or man,
Embracing all parts of you, in your entirety,
Is the epitome of beauty, it's true sincerity.

Vulnerability allows you to connect,
With yourself and others, to truly reflect,
The beauty of self-love shines bright,
In vulnerability, it's a beautiful sight.

9. THE STRENGTH OF SELF-LOVE IN BOUNDARIES

Self-love empowers you to erect firm boundaries,
Shielding yourself from those who try to trespass with impunity.
It imbues you with the resilience to endure,
Even in the most daunting circumstances, maintaining your sovereignty.

It emboldens you to remain steadfast in your convictions,
True to your beliefs and what you hold dear.
It also compels you to detach from those who don't honour your restrictions,
Realizing their toxicity isn't worth holding near.

Remember that self-love isn't about being perfect or selfish,
It's about valuing and protecting yourself, just like you would a friend.
So, embrace your worth and set those boundaries,
And watch how much stronger you become in the end.

10. NAVIGATING RELATIONSHIPS WITH SELF-LOVE

There was a time when
I'd sacrifice my all for love's sake,
But now I've learned that self-love is no mistake.
I used to always say yes, afraid to decline,
But now I'm confident in my limits, and my boundaries are just fine.

Once I thought self-love was just being selfish and vain,
But now I know it's necessary for my mental health and inner pain.
I used to dim my light so others wouldn't feel insecure,
But now I shine bright and proudly, and it's their turn to endure.

Before, I would stay silent to avoid a heated fray,
But now I speak up and own my needs, come what may.
I'd give the silent treatment and play push-and-pull games,
But now I stand firm in my worth, with no one else to blame.

I used to search for love from all the wrong places,
But now I find it within myself, in the most meaningful spaces.
I blamed others for my emptiness and felt unlovable and flawed,
But now I accept myself fully, and my love is self-awed.

It wasn't easy accepting myself and feeling my emotions too,
But now I know it's vital to living an authentic life, honest and true.
I used to expect others to fulfill my every need,
But now I'm self-reliant and fulfilled, and that's all I need to succeed.

And when someone rejects me, I no longer question my worth,
I understand that love isn't one-sided and it takes mutual effort to birth.
Self-love is the only key to change relationship dynamics,
To create meaningful connections, and navigate life's enigmatic antics.

It's only through self-love that we can accept others and their flaws,
And that's the foundation for a relationship that endures all its gnarly jaws.
For it takes courage to love ourselves and others as they are,
But the result is a relationship that can withstand even the toughest scar.

7

Cultivating Self-Love as a Daily Practice

1. DAILY SELF-LOVE PRACTICE

S elf-love is key, it's true to say,
It should be practiced every single day.
Connect with yourself in various ways,
Through mindfulness, meditation, or exercises always.

Express yourself with writing, let your creativity flow,
Or take a walk in nature to stay grounded and grow.
Surround yourself with those who uplift and inspire,
And connect with the Divine Source to rise higher.

Don't forget your inner child, let playfulness take hold,
And commit to yourself first, before others you unfold.
Listen to your inner voice, it knows what's right,
Speak up when needed, and be silent when it's right.

Do something each day that brings you joy,
And learn new things to expand your employ.
Love yourself in challenges, through thick and thin,
Be kind to yourself, and let self-compassion win.

Let go of control, it only holds you back,
Make peace with your inner critic, and cut yourself some slack.
My dear friend, choose self-love every day,
Until it becomes a part of you, in every single way.

2. THE FEELING OF CONFIDENCE

When daily self-love becomes your way,
Fearless decisions come into play,
Your body feels lighter, with no dismay,
Belongingness grows in every way.

In the moment, you joyfully sway,
With calmness and confidence at bay,
Embrace the world as you are today,
Daily self-love is the only way.

With each practice, emotions soar,
Feelings of worth you can't ignore,
Self-love's power opens every door,
A life of fulfillment to explore.

So, embrace yourself, love every part,
Daily self-love is where you start,
The journey to a happy heart,
Self-love is the most beautiful art.

Remember, it's not just a trend,
A way of life, your heart to mend,
With daily self-love, you'll ascend,
To happiness that never ends.

3. SELF-LOVE GARDEN

Self-love is like tending to a garden fair,
Water it daily with tender care.
Just like your self needs nurturing too,
Some parts are more fragile, some less so true.

Listen to triggers, work on them well,
And tend to your strengths, give them a swell.
Patience is key in both plant and soul,
To germinate, grow, and reach your goal.

The garden brings peace, grounds your mind,
Similarly, stay grounded, and be kind.
Love and passion, both in garden and heart,
Will make your life bloom, a work of art.

4. MAKE SELF-LOVE A PRIORITY

Make self-love your daily call,
Else you'll feel disconnected, lose it all,
Worldly visions will sweep you away,
And never will you feel fulfilled each day.

Forgetting values, boundaries blurred,
Pursuing dreams will seem absurd,
Accept life's flow with love in your heart,
Else resentful, not grateful, you'll fall apart.

From deep within, love others too,
But without self-love, it can't be true,
Happiness and fulfillment, out of sight,
Without self-love, life loses its light.

5. CONSISTENCY IN PRACTICING SELF-LOVE

To find inner peace, self-love is a must,
Consistency is key, in yourself you must trust,
Happiness is within, if you practice each day,
Fulfillment will come if you don't stray.

It's not natural for us to love ourselves,
Our narratives must change, like books on shelves,
Reprograming our minds takes effort and time,
But with consistency, we'll feel sublime.

Choosing to love oneself each day,
Is a choice that we all must make our way,
With consistent practice, you'll unleash your power,
And become whole within, a blooming flower.

So don't give up, keep going strong,
Consistency will lead you where you belong,
With determination and effort, you will be,
The best version of yourself, just wait and see!

6. BENEFITS OF DAILY SELF-LOVE

Self-love can truly be a game-changer,
In ways that you might not expect,
Your connection with yourself grows stronger,
And with others, you're more correct.

Compassion flows, both inward and out,
Imperfections don't make you feel low,
You embrace yourself, without a doubt,
And accept others as they grow.

As confidence rises, you shine,
And your best self shows up each day,
No more self-sabotage, it's time,
To live in the present and play.

Happiness comes from deep inside,
Not from what others might say,
Your worth is not something you hide,
It's intrinsic, and here to stay.

Validation isn't what you seek,
Your authentic self is enough,
Healthy boundaries help you not be meek,
And your service to others is tough.

Relationships become more profound,
As you build connections with care,

With self-love, your life becomes unbound,
And harmonious, beyond compare.

7. SELF-LOVE FEELING

Self-love's a feeling I adore,
Spreading through me, to my core,
Like the light that enters through my crown,
And runs through every fiber down.

It touches atoms, molecules small,
Deep and expansive, covering all,
Filling me with happiness and glee,
A sense of joy that's truly free.

It opens up my wings to fly,
A feeling of power, oh so high,
All-encompassing love flows in,
And out, freeing me from within.

This surreal sense of belonging,
Fulfills me, with love, it's thronging,
No other feeling can compare,
This sense of fulfillment is rare and fair.

8. TALE OF MY JOURNEY

This is the tale,
Of my journey to unveil,
The importance of self-love,
And how it transformed my life above.

Once I sought love outside,
In people, places, and achievements I tried,
But it was like chasing the wind,
A love that could never truly begin.

My past kept pointing to me,
Through the ups and downs, it was clear to see,
I learned to be a parent to my inner child,
With self-love, I found my spirit running wild.

Learning self-love was not easy,
In the beginning, it felt messy and breezy,
Stepping out of my comfort zone,
Shedding inadequacies, I've known.

Letting go of control and being right,
Required consistent practice and might,
After coming home to myself,
I learned to love my true self.

No more chasing love outside of me,
I am whole within and free,
Whatever I do, I do it with love in my heart,
Passionate about my dreams, I follow my part.

Transforming within transforms me without,
No more dimming my light to make others comfortable or devout,
With my flaws and all, I shine my light bright,
Unstoppable me, ready for any fight.

Transformation happens from within,
Manifesting in my reality, a new world to begin,
No more scared of my full potential to see,
Self-love is my daily practice, and I am finally free.

9. SELF-LOVE AND SELF-CARE

When you prioritize your own self-care,
Your understanding of yourself becomes more clear.
You discover what makes you happy, and not,
And you're more aware of the emotions you've got.

You learn what triggers you, and where you feel,
You recognize who resonates, and who isn't real.
You release the need to take things personally,
And focus on healing wounds and traumas, sincerely.

You accept yourself, flaws and all,
And forgive the past, no need to fall.
You shift from blame to an inner game,
Developing self-compassion without shame.

You know what works for you, and what does not,
And prioritize your own needs, giving it a shot.
You show the world how you deserve to be treated,
And commit to keeping your promises, not defeated.

You come home to your own self-love,
Like siblings from the same mother, above.
Self-care and self-love are intertwined,
Nurturing both, to a healthy state of mind.

10. SELF-LOVE AND POSITIVITY

When self-love fills up your heart,
You're ready for a brand-new start,
Your breathing's deep, your muscles loose,
Relaxed, at ease, no need to choose.

Connecting with others, it's a breeze,
Your positivity's sure to please,
You take imperfect actions, every day,
Inspired and confident, come what may.

All emotions, you embrace with care,
Silencing negative talk, without despair,
Walking tall, talking bold,
Self-assurance and trust, take hold.

Unleashing your potential, all the way,
Following your heart, with no delay,
In stillness and solitude, you'll find,
Happiness within, with peace of mind.

With a sense of freedom, pure and true,
Being yourself, is all you need to do,
Filled with love, and positivity,
Your body's calm, in pure serenity.

8

Healing and Moving Forward with Self-Love

1. THE HEALING POWER OF SELF-LOVE

Self-love is a balm that mends past wounds,
It's the key to all our answers, attuned,
A melody of soothing to our pain,
And a way to rewrite our past stories again.

It's the strength to speak up and stand tall,
To let go of what no longer serves us at all,
To set boundaries that keep us safe,
And to embrace our imperfections with grace.

It unleashes our potential, boosts confidence too,
And helps us trust in ourselves anew,
Self-love's a tool of healing power,
It transforms us, and blossoms like a flower.

So, let's love ourselves, every part,
And heal our wounds with a gentle heart,
For in our self-love, we'll find the way,
To overcome all that's held us astray.

2. THE FEELING OF HEALING WITH SELF-LOVE

I feel the healing, as I move ahead with love for me,
When the butterflies subside, and my heart's no longer in agony,
The turmoil in my gut's at ease, and my knees don't ache,
My spleen is joyful, and I don't take things to heart, for heaven's sake!

I let go of people and stories that don't serve my growth,
I don't fear rejection or proving my worth, my worth's my oath,
Validation is no longer my aim, my peace is my own,
I face my pain, sit with it, and overcome it alone.

No distractions, no numbing, nor projecting, I bear the pain,
Talking to it helps me heal, and I'm not afraid to take the reins,
I move forward, with love and care, toward a brighter day,
And in this healing journey, I find a better way.

The smell of fresh air fills my lungs, as I breathe with ease,
My vision's clear, my heart's light, as if a burden lifted, if you please,
The sound of silence, so serene, as I revel at the moment,
My senses are alive, I'm truly grateful, this healing's no mere atonement.

With each step forward, my soul shines, brighter than before,
I'm not the same person, and that's alright, I don't need to ignore,
My past, my pain, and my fears, they've shaped me into who I am,
And I'll keep moving forward, with self-love, as my guiding hand.

3. HEALING WITH SELF-LOVE IS LIKE A JOURNEY

The journey of healing,
Is like the lava in a cocoon
That transforms to a butterfly,
It's a metamorphosis that happens soon.

It's not an easy road to travel,
With thousands of falls on the way,
It takes strength to rise each time,
And consistent practice every day.

It requires the courage to face the darkness,
And patience to purify and cleanse,
Like a seed that germinates slowly,
Before it blossoms with elegance.

The process of healing takes time,
With destruction, renewal, and reset,
It requires rebuilding what's broken,
And loads of patience, don't forget.

It takes years of solitude,
And being misunderstood too,
Like a baby in the mother's womb,
Before birth, it takes time to renew.

Moving forward with self-love,
Takes you away from the world outside,
In a hermit mode, to know yourself,
And trust the unknown, to confide.

Complete trust in the process,
Like a baby that knows it's provided for,
It's painful, messy, and challenging,
But worth it, to open up love's door.

The journey of healing is like a voyage,
With highs and lows, moments of tears,
It's a journey of self-discovery,
That helps conquer all fears.

4. SELF-LOVE IS THE KEY

Love yourself, it's the key,
To heal and grow, just wait and see,
Without self-love, it's hard to progress,
Your growth and healing won't be at their best.

Self-love can help you reach new heights,
Your progress will be swift and bright,
Without it, you'll always feel incomplete,
Like a puzzle missing a crucial piece.

Boost your ego, prove your worth,
But deep down, it's just a show of your hurt,
Only with self-love will you truly know,
Your roots, your patterns, and where you'll go.

Embrace all parts of you, even the flaws,
Your healing process will have no pause,
Compassion and forgiveness come with ease,
As you grow and heal, your soul will be pleased.

So, love yourself, and watch how you thrive,
Your personal growth will come alive,
Self-love is the key to heal and grow,
Embrace it, and watch your spirit glow.

5. SELF-LOVE FOR HEALING

To heal your wounds and ease your pain,
Self-love must be your constant refrain.
It's the tool that speeds up the process,
A way to unburden and find progress.

When you become aware of the stories you tell,
The ones that kept you stuck in a spell,
You realize the chains were all an illusion,
And the love you seek is your own solution.

Self-love allows you to care for your own needs,
And from your overflow, others' hearts you can feed.
You embrace every part of who you are,
Finding your projections and the pieces afar.

Judgment and negativity, start to fade,
As self-love is the choice you've made.
Rewriting your narrative, you take conscious action,
The stories we tell, have a profound impact.

We are all stories we believe in,
And self-love is the way to begin.
You become mindful of your emotions and feelings,
As self-love makes your healing journey appealing.

So, dear one, take a deep breath and start,
Embrace the love within your heart,

For you are worthy of all the love and care,
And with self-love, your soul can rep.

6. SELF-LOVE AND FORGIVENESS

Self-love and forgiveness are intertwined,
A connection that's easy to find,
When you embrace who you truly are,
The truth shines through like a shining star.

Unfulfilled lives can hold us back,
But self-love helps us get back on track,
We see the root cause of our pain,
And find the strength to love again.

Forgiving ourselves is the key,
To setting our own hearts free,
And once we've found that sweet release,
We can forgive others with ease.

For what we give ourselves is what we give,
To others, so let's learn to live,
With love and kindness in our hearts,
And watch as healing truly starts.

The connection between self-love and forgiveness,
Is powerful and full of promise,
So, let's embrace it with open arms,
And find the peace that it imparts.

7. FREEDOM FROM PAST HURTS

Self-love is powerful, it's hard to describe,
It starts with awakening, no need to hide,
Past hurts arise, demanding justice and revenge,
Blame and anger, seeking to avenge.

But as I delve deeper, understanding who I am,
Acceptance and love, like an internal program,
I see the hurtful impressions, I've carried within,
Forgiveness for myself, a new journey begins.

Others who caused pain, I forgive and understand,
Their actions were not about me, but their own internal band,
It frees me from the weight, of all past hurts and pain,
Liberated like a bird, no longer restrained.

A feeling of freedom, from limiting beliefs and thought,
Like waves washing burdens away, the feeling can't be bought,
I'm light and clear, like light passing through,
A feeling so wonderful, like the sky so blue.

8. SELF-LOVE STRENGTHENS

Once unfulfilled, lost, and unwell,
My spirit, mind, and soul did rebel,
Emotions scattered, haywire they fell,
Resentment, anger, and anxiety swelled.

My identity is tied to others' needs,
A fixer and a savior for all to heed,
Seeking love and validation, my heart did plead,
Forgetting my own self, my soul did bleed.

Charity and service I gave for free,
Not valuing my worth, I couldn't see,
Fear of missing out blinded me,
Lost in the chaos, my body had to plea.

To go within, to sit and feel,
All the pain that I tried to conceal,
Digging deeper, the truth revealed,
The love I lacked, I had to steal.

From within, I gave myself to care,
Healing faster, with a love so rare,
Creativity blossomed, beyond compare,
With empathy and compassion, I learned to share.

Forgiving myself, not taking things personally,
My strength emerged, from a place so early,

Overcoming past challenges, so thoroughly,
With self-love, I'm now one, so surely.

9. HEALING EMPOWERS

The joy of healing, it's truly thrilling,
With self-love, the power's fulfilling.
I feel alive, like a blooming flower,
Moving forward with my newfound power.

My heart is full, my mind is clear,
No more self-doubt, no more fear.
I'm confident in who I am,
Empowered by my own self-love jam.

Compassion and love fill my soul,
A sense of peace that makes me whole.
I feel positive and free,
With a clear vision of who I can be.

The joy of freedom, it's hard to explain,
The power of healing has cured my pain.
Being empowered from within,
Is the best feeling, let the healing begin.

10. POWER OF A COMMUNITY

In the arms of those who care,
I find the strength to heal and repair.
There's power in this community,
One that I'm proud to be a part of, you see.

Surrounded by love and support so true,
I feel safe, I feel seen, I feel anew.
They understand my struggles and pain,
And hold space for me to feel it again.

These like-minded souls resonate with my heart,
As we journey together, never to be apart.
They accept all of me, the good and the bad,
And give me the assurance that I won't be had.

With them, I feel my dreams take flight,
Guided in the right direction, towards the light.
They stand beside me when I stumble and fall,
And lift me up, so I can stand tall.

Their presence is a balm to my soul,
And their love for me; makes me whole.
I cherish these people who love me for me,
For they are the ones who set me free.

Their support is a gift beyond measure,
A treasure to hold onto and to treasure.

With them, I can move forward with love,
And heal from the pain that once felt like a glove.

If you too need people who care,
Find your community and know they'll be there.
With them by your side, you'll never be alone,
And together, you'll create a heart-warming home

Conclusion: Embracing Your Authentic Self

1. CELEBRATING AUTHENTICITY

Like a rainbow's hues so bright,
Authenticity shines with might.
It means embracing all your songs,
And celebrating past mistakes as gongs.

Celebrate all that you're blessed with,
Including parts you once suppressed.
The beauty of your shape and size,
Shouldn't conform to others' lies.

Embrace your ignorance with glee,
And weaknesses too, for they make thee.

Celebrate all emotions true,
And who you were, and are anew.

Let your colors boldly show,
As you grow into you, you know.
Authenticity is a prize,
And celebrating it, is truly wise.

2. STRENGTH IN VULNERABILITY

Your strength will bloom when you are true,
When you show the world what's really you.
It's okay to be seen as weak,
And let others see the tears you leak.

You'll find true power when you're real,
Not just putting on a polished appeal.
Don't do things just for love and praise,
But because it's what your heart portrays.

No secrets hidden, no mask to wear,
Your true self is what you'll share.
Flaunt your flaws as much as your strengths,
And embrace the journey, at any length.

It takes courage to be vulnerable,
To let your guard down and show your label.
But there's so much strength in authenticity,
A poetic journey to find serenity.

3. MIRROR OF REFLECTION

Gazing in the mirror of self-reflection,
Can send shivers down your spine,
But take a glance,
And witness parts of you that you've yet to find.

Face the mirror with bravery,
Embrace yourself in full,
Accept all that you see,
Even the parts that make you feel dull.

It may not be a simple task,
But it will come from deep within,
With practice and persistence,
Authenticity will soon begin.

Repetition is the key,
To learn and grow strong,
Repeat until it's a part of thee,
And your true self will belong.

For the mirror is a tool,
That holds the power of your soul,
The reflection it shows is true,
And it will help you reach your goal.

4. CELEBRATE YOUR AUTHENTIC VOICE

Oh, how melodious the sound,
Of your authentic voice profound,
Sweet words flowing true and free,
Like music from a symphony.

Some may not understand your song,
But those meant to will sing along,
The music of authenticity,
Is a powerful force of positivity.

It soothes and calms; inspires and excites,
Triggers feelings that take flight,
Opens up the soul, unlocks the heart,
Brings out gifts that were once apart.

No one can speak or sing like you,
No one can bring out the truth as true,
You inspire, activate, and manifest,
With a voice that's truly blessed.

The power within your unique voice,
Is a gift that is yours to rejoice,
Keep speaking from your authentic core,
Inspiring others forevermore.

Keep singing from your heart and soul,
Celebrating your voice, let it unfold,

The music of authenticity; is oh-so-sweet.
A melody that's uniquely complete.

5. PATH TO SELF-DISCOVERY

To find yourself, embrace authenticity,
It's the key to unlocking self-discovery,
Be honest and stop running away,
From your feelings that hold so much sway.

Don't speak just to please others' whims,
Nor seek validation or approval from him or her or them,
Face your inner critic and the voice of not enough,
To know yourself better, it's a must.

Don't blame others, take responsibility,
For the truth, face it with humility,
Embrace your imperfections, don't push them away
Stop self-sabotaging and find happiness every day

Accept all flaws and past mistakes,
Forgive yourself, for your own sake,
Practice gratitude, make it a daily ritual,
Seek your unmet needs within, it's not trivial.

Befriend your shadow self, don't deny,
It's a part of you, don't let it make you shy,
This journey's tough, but it's worth the strife,
The path to self-discovery is the only way to life.

6. LIBERATION OF AUTHENTICITY

As I embrace my truest form,
I feel a sense of being reborn,
Freedom and empowerment flow,
Gratitude and forgiveness grow.

Acceptance fills me to the core,
Lightness lifts me up and more,
Confidence blossoms from within,
Wholeness reigns, a brand-new skin.

Appreciation for who I am,
Seen and heard, no need to cram,
Spirit soars, reaching new heights,
Vision expands; a brand-new sight.

Clarity clears the foggy view,
Blissfulness, a feeling anew,
This liberation, a journey to take,
Authenticity is the path to make.

So let go of fear and be true,
The power is within you too,
Liberate yourself, break free
Authenticity is the key to see.

7. AUTHENTICITY AND INNER LIGHT

Embrace authenticity, let your light shine bright,
Imperfections and mistakes, don't put up a fight,
Unleash your power, let love flow from within,
Flaws and uniqueness, let your soul begin.

Your voice is unique, use it to soothe,
Inspire others to shine, don't be aloof,
Speak the truth, show up as you are,
Attract true souls, like a shining star.

Touch the souls of others, open the vault of light,
Let authenticity guide you, with all your might,
Be true to yourself, let your light shine through,
The world needs your authenticity, it's up to you.

8. IN THE GARDEN OF AUTHENTICITY

In the Garden of Authenticity,
Plants and flowers bloom with serenity,
No comparisons, no envy,
Just embracing their own identity.

Each one shines in its own right,
Nurturing itself with all its might,
Without a gardener's touch in sight,
It blossoms, grows, and takes flight.

Just like the plants, we too must see,
The beauty of our authenticity,
Nurture it every single day,
And let it shine in every way.

Choose to be true, choose to be real,
Embrace your quirks, let them reveal,
The garden of authenticity, it's surreal,
With every crooked stem, it still appeals.

Let's cultivate our truest form,
Without trying to conform,
In the Garden of Authenticity,
We can truly weather any storm.

9. THE ART OF AUTHENTICITY

Embrace your authenticity, don't be a copy,
You're a rare gem, like no other floppy,
You're beautiful, smart, and quite intelligent,
Your kindness and patience, are always evident.

Talented in ways that are all your own,
Don't dim your light, don't ever postpone,
Your dance or song may be offbeat,
But you shine in a way that's truly unique.

Embrace all aspects of who you are,
The good, the bad, and the things that leave a scar,
Discover your true self, don't try to hide,
Embrace self-love, let it be your guide.

Take care of yourself, your mind, and your soul
Your individuality should always be your goal
The art of authenticity is a journey within
So, embrace it all, and let your true self win.

10. A TAPESTRY OF AUTHENTICITY

I celebrate my authenticity, a tapestry of threads so fine,
Once silenced, now I revel in my unique voice divine,
My body, a vessel for my soul, a wondrous gift,
To experience life's highs and lows, and all its twists and rifts.

I celebrate my shapes and sizes, a diversity so grand,
And dress in ways that showcase; my individual brand,
My laughter, a melody, a tune that's mine alone,
Intelligence and perspectives are all uniquely my own.

My focus, my creativity, and my traits; are all one-of-a-kind,
Talkative, moody, and regulating myself, I don't mind,
Studying human behavior, my passion, my pursuit,
Areas of ignorance, weaknesses, my attributes not mute.

Mistakes, a teacher, make me wiser and strong,
Sensuality, sexuality, I celebrate all along,
Heart, soul, light, and temperaments, all facets of me,
My shadows, my truth, and my values are all a part of my tapestry.

Younger versions, future ones, all integral to my being,
For I am not just some parts, nor limited by what I'm seeing,
Beyond concepts, I am, formless and form,
Celebrating all of me, in this tapestry, I conform not to any norm.

Deep within my heart's embrace,
A gentle whisper finds its place,
A voice that sings of love and light,
Of healing and renewal bright.

It guides me on a journey true,
A path that's meant for you and me,
To discover the love within,
The essence of who we've always been.

This is the call for Self-Love,
A radiant awakening from above.

Resources

These are a few of the books and courses that have helped me understand Self-Love better and to experience it and integrate it into my personal journey of healing and growth.

1. Salzberg, Sharon. Real Love: The Art of Mindful Connection. Flatiron Books, 2017.

2. Hay, Louise. You Can Heal Your Life. Hay House, 1984.

3. Sincero, Jen. You Are a Badass: How to Stop Doubting Your Greatness and Start Living an Awesome Life. Running Press, 2013.

4. Pueblo, Yung. Lighter: Let Go of the Past, Connect with the Present,

5. and Expand the Future. Andrews McMeel Publishing, 2020.

6. Angelou, Maya. And Still, I Rise, Random,House, 1978.

7. Shetty, Jay. 8 Rules of Love: How to Find It, Keep It, and Let It Go. Simon & Schuster, 2023.

8. Ravikant, Kamal. Love Yourself Like Your Life Depends on It. CreateSpace Independent Publishing Platform, 2012.

9. Godfred, Melody. Self-Love Poetry: For Thinkers and Feelers. Thought Catalog Books, 2020.

10. Kiloby, Scott. Love's Quiet Revolution: The End of the Spiritual Search. New Harbinger Publications, 2018.

11. Kiloby, Scott. Living Realization: A Simple, Plain-English Guide to Non-Duality. Kiloby Publications, 2015.

12. Peer, Marisa. I Am Enough: Mark Your Mirror and Change Your Life. Hay House UK, 2019.

13. Anderson, Marisa. Ultimate Confidence: The Secret to Feeling Great About Yourself Every Day. Capstone, 2012.

14. Uncompromised Life by Marissa Peer (Mindvalley Quest)

15. The Integral Life by Ken Wilber (Mindvalley Quest)

16. Live by your own Rules by Kristina Mand-Lakhiani (Mindvalley Quest)

17. Total Self-Confidence by Paul McKenna (Mindvalley Quest)

Acknowledgment

I express my gratitude to the Universe, My Divine Self, **Grand Master Choa Kok Sui**, All My Spiritual Teachers, My Ancestors, My Spirit Guides, and all the Holy Ones for flowing through me and allowing me to serve as a channel for sharing love through this book.

I am grateful to my husband **Somchandra Nahakpam** for being a pillar of support, for stepping in to take care of responsibilities in my absence, and for providing ideas and suggestions that have contributed to the success of this book. Without your love and support, this journey would not have been possible, nor would this book have come to fruition.

My daughter **Lamyanbi Nahakpam** deserves special recognition for her unwavering support and sacrifice of time to help me complete this book. Without her love and understanding, writing and completing this book would have been an insurmountable task.

I am thankful to my younger brother **Rajiv Irungbam** for being my companion, providing valuable insights and suggestions regarding the book title and other aspects, and supporting me in numerous ways. Without your presence, this journey would have been lonely and arduous.

I extend my gratitude to my **Parents** for giving me life and nurturing me into the person I am today, as well as to my **Sisters** for being a source of strength.

I am indebted to my coach **Sombathla** for his tremendous influence in teaching me the right tools and techniques, and for introducing me to a world of possibilities in pursuing my dream of becoming a writer, not only in India but globally. This book would not have reached the world without you.

I express my appreciation to my **AFH** community, my **Team Supernova**, and our facilitator **Manjul Tiwari** for their support, guidance, and constructive feedback.

I am grateful to my friend **Mandeep Bachheta** for always believing in my dream to write a book, encouraging me to follow my soul's calling, and setting an example by stepping into her own power.

I thank my friend and painting teacher **Diganta Dutta** for teaching me to connect with my creative soul, to not only paint better but also to write better, and also for supporting me in spreading words about my book.

I extend my appreciation to **Preethi Byrappa, Monita Nanjappa, Keerthana Gopal, Preetha, Karuna Irungbam, Amit Mehta, Gauri Mahajan, Neha Makkar, Ramesh Dubey, Dipin Chachlani, Deepthi, Sushmita Shetty, Piku, Palei, Pinky Naorem, Deepak, Jiten, Sophia Laimayum, Sanchita Das and Shanthalembi** for their support and trust in my work. Their encouragement has given me the confidence to follow another dream and complete this second book.

I would also like to acknowledge all my friends, family, relatives, and colleagues whose names I may have missed, but whose help and support have been invaluable, like Earth Angels.

I express my gratitude to all the coaches, authors, and healers whose books, courses, and healings have inspired, healed, and transformed my life and the lives of countless others.

I acknowledge the work of Mindvalley in transforming millions of lives and raising the collective consciousness.

I thank **Sooraj Achar(#1_BestSeller)**, for formatting my book and leading me through some of the last steps before my book got published.

I extend my thanks to my graphic designer and editor for making this book beautiful and presentable.

Finally, I express my heartfelt gratitude to all my readers for trusting in my work and supporting me. Without you, this book that I have written would have been nothing more than a showpiece.

145

About Author

V elory Irungbam, Author of "**Awakening to Self-Love**"

Velory Irungbam is a full-time mother, loving wife, and writer from Manipur, currently residing in Mumbai, India with her family. She holds a Master's degree in Social Work and has served the people of Manipur as a **Block Health Program Manager** in NRHM, Ministry of Health and Family Welfare, for several years. However, her commitment to transformation and healing led her to pursue a **Ph.D.** in Public Health at TISS, Mumbai, which she later dropped out to become a full-time mother and follow her soul purpose.

Velory is passionate about transforming herself and others; and has learned various methods such as Pranic Healing, Akashic Record Reading, and other courses at Mindvalley. Currently, she is also pursuing painting and sketching to enhance her creativity, which helps convey her thoughts and emotions in writing.

Her writings and creative works are an embodiment of her soul's purpose, which is to help others heal and raise the collective consciousness. **Velory** is an advocate of empowering individuals to follow their dreams, embrace their true selves, and make positive changes in their lives.

Recently, **Velory Irungbam** published her first poetry book, **"Feel, Flow and Heal to Meet Thyself,"** on Amazon.in, where she encourages readers to embrace their emotions and connect with their inner selves to heal and transform from within.

In summary, **Velory Irungbam** is a talented artist, healer, writer, and aspiring transformational coach, dedicated to inspiring and empowering others. Her journey serves as a reminder that self-discovery and growth are lifelong pursuits, and that pursuing your dreams is never too late.

Contact Velory at -

veloryirungbam@gmail.com

facebook.com/velory.irungbam?mibextid=ZbWKwL

https://instagram.com/velirungbam?igshid=ZDdkNTZiNTM=

Printed in Great Britain
by Amazon